New Online
GRAMMAR

For Today's Writing

Writing Tips, Techniques & Shortcuts to Influence and Motivate Online

D.R. Martin, PhD*
(*Personal human Development)

SmartyPants Press
Falmouth, Maine 04105
www.SmartyPantsSecrets.com

ISBN 13: 978-1-943971-00-8
ISBN 10: 1943971005

Copyright 2015 D.R. Martin, PhD*
(*Personal human Development)

The SmartyPants Secrets Concept

A **SmartyPants Secret** is that **one piece of information** that you need to know to make every job a little bit, or maybe a lot, **easier**. Almost everything we do in life has a SmartyPants secret that to it, that knowing the "secret" would help tremendously in shortening the learning curve.

After experiencing many "a ha!" moments that were previous head bangers, I realized that there was a lot of grief – i.e. aggravation, wasted time, spent resources - that could have been saved if I had known to tap into the insider information that others had and I was lacking. A SmartyPants secret is that crucial bit of timely knowledge.

We all want a magic bullet answer that solves all of our problems in one fell swoop and makes everything go perfectly well, preferably in record time! We want that magic to happen right NOW, to be easily done, and to be preferably cheap, or at least not at great expense. There are a lot of demands on our unattainable magic ☺

For example, one day I looked at my face and damn if I didn't see a "sun spot" (nastily also called a "liver" spot) marring the surface of my otherwise smooth face on the right lower cheek. I scheduled an appointment at the dermatologist to verify the find and see if it could be lasered off. She sent me to an aesthetician who gave me some key information that made a huge difference in my decision of what to do next.

I was told that my even slightly darker (Asian) skin carries more pigment than Caucasian skin obviously. But what's not obvious is the way the body works, specifically the way the skin works, which is that when you wound the skin's surface, which laser surgery would certainly do, extra pigments rush to the spot to heal it (the "job" of pigment is to protect the underlying cells). The net result is that non-Caucasian skin heals into darker scabs and scars. (I have noticed this phenomena before but never made a direct connection.) Why then would I ever choose to have laser surgery on my face to remove a mark only to end up with an even darker mark? Yikes!

Obviously I wouldn't, but without this specialized knowledge about different results with different skin types, that even the dermatologist didn't know (yes, she was the recommender of the laser surgery option) I would've made a poor decision, with permanent negative results. A SmartyPants timely secret to the rescue!

Experts, who have hours of experience doing what the newbie is attempting to do, have expert knowledge, which may not be so secret, but it is **key information** that the novice greatly needs.

If you've ever struggled with something then learned the 'something' afterwards that caused you to say to yourself or to say aloud, "*Well, **if I only known THAT before I did this**, it would've made a world of difference!*" then you just learned a SmartyPants secret - the hard way.

The short SmartyPants Secrets books give you the secret that you need on a given topic, the most important piece of information that makes the greatest difference between easier success and hard-fought failure.

When I was young there was a professor at Cornell University, which in his obituary listed him as "***the last man to know*** *everything*." I was taken by the concept of anyone knowing everything there is to know contained in one brain. Oh, to have such a mind!

But **to know everything**, logical facts and figures, and **to be able to do everything** are **two different things**. Brain power doesn't equal skill and expertise.

Today that one brain that knows everything is the Internet. There is so much information today available on the Internet; we can all be like that professor at Cornell and have access to all knowledge at the click of our fingertips.

More knowledge than we could ever consume - **who has time** to go through it all? Most of the time **what you really want is to know is the crux of the subject** on hand, not the whole litany of everything imaginable that is available to know.

Tell me just what I need to know! (and I likely don't know what specific knowledge to ask for). It's literally impossible to know what you don't know. Let the expertise of knowledgeable others guide you.

If you are new to a topic the **SmartyPants secret can save you time and effort**, which are important to your success. Not a complete course on the topic, which you can certainly get elsewhere, the SmartyPants secrets concept is primarily to help you **not miss the key information needed for success**.

The building block of knowledge that the foundation rests upon; the Keystone or cornerstone knowledge makes a critical difference, especially when that knowledge that you do have, or think you have, is **faulty, incomplete or missing** entirely.

The concept of **social proof** states that when we have no prior experience in a given situation we rely on **others to show us the way**. We believe that lacking personal knowledge, that their situation is similar to our situation, and therefore what worked for them has a high probability of working for us.

We quiz others about our shared

circumstances around the situation to verify that their solution is a good one. Plus, we think: *there's nothing to lose in trying since I don't have a better answer.*

Then when what worked for another doesn't happen to work for us, we are reminded that **we are all different people**, with different variables that impact success or failure. Some solutions to problems are hit or miss depending on who we are. And sometimes success depends on having and following the right key knowledge.

Solving problems is not the complete SmartyPants concept, although SmartyPants secrets can indeed offer real help for real problems. Rather the full concept is that having that key knowledge piece makes efforts easier and successful quicker; hopefully **avoiding having the problem in the first place**. We do anything in life because we have a goal to achieve. Reaching that goal successfully, quickly and easier than without knowing the SmartPants secret is the SmartyPants concept.

And because **all SmartyPants secrets have a physiological root**, grounded in our shared human biology, every SmartyPants secret is valid for everyone, no matter who you are. While we are all uniquely different from each other, we have a **common biology** consisting of inherited traits that stretch back to the Neanderthal era.

Applying a SmartyPants secret **will work for you no matter who you are**. And in our busy world, who doesn't want to save time and know the SmartyPants secret to anything?

Why ever risk hindering easier success by not knowing the core success secret?

New Online GRAMMAR

A Quick Cruise Through New Online Grammar Rules, and Getting Attention Online

In the Age of the Internet, Embrace New Grammar Rules (yay!)

We are living in the 21st century where communication has moved heavily online. And with the new age comes new grammar rules. The grammar fanatics of the past may be aghast, but that's the reality. Living language changes and we need to keep up with the times.

The advice is not to throw all old grammar rules. You need to know the old standards to veer from them, so the strict thinkers will be delighted to know that much of the basics - will be covered in the SmartyPants cruise through the formal world of high grammar.

New grammar rules help to get online attention, to get noticed amidst the noisy internet, so our important message can *stand out from the crowd* in the new world of online writing that we are in today.

New Grammar Rules

RULE Hyper Grammar - ignore pundits who call you out on correctness

Hyper grammar – who needs it?

All those corrections: *"that's not really grammatically correct"* are a thing of the past. We are now in the new age of: If it sounds right to most people, it's in common usage, then it IS right, so go ahead and use it!

Remember: **"Who Do You Trust?"**

Who Do You Trust? was an old TV show emceed by Johnny Carson in the late 1950's, with a grammatically incorrect title - it should have been: "**WHOM** *Do You Trust?"*

But even 60 years ago the lexicon was

12

changing and the producers knew that 'whom' was being replaced slowly but surely by 'who'. It's more natural.

*"Knock, knock...**who**'s there?"* (not: ***"Whom** is there?")*

***"Who**'s calling?"* (the 'proper', stilted version is: *"To **whom** am I speaking?")*

We used to have grammatical fistfights over *"It's **me**"* (arguably correct as: *"It is **I**")*

A really old-fashioned favorite expression: *"Woe is **me**!"* (which is more grammatically correct as: *"Woe is **I**!")*

Since no one says *"Woe is me"* anymore, as the word 'woe' is woefully unused these days, the very grammatically correct *"Woe is unto me"* should bury that expression completely in the grave.

For 4 decades, the grammar on Neil Armstrong's famous quote has been argued:

"That's one small step for man, one giant leap for mankind"

In response, let's all add a resounding: *who cares about this grammar?* Stop the grammar argument - Let it go already!

What difference does it really make whether there should be an "a" in front of "man", or not (with "man" representing humanity)? C'mon, grammar geeks, we get it, but the meaning of the idea doesn't change, no matter the grammar. And the way Neil said it just flows better, has better construction balance to the ear.

The new grammar rules called for a relaxation of hyper grammar. Let the old school teachers wag their finger at the sliding language of the Internet generation, in favor of the friendliness of **common usage**.

Hoot note: *If everyone else is saying it a certain way and it sounds right, then it IS right. Better to be like everyone else and grammatically wrong, but socially right.*

RULE: SPELLING always counts, so always get the spelling right

Real headline: *"Advertisers are not responsible for mistakes maked by this publication."*
(duh, no staff proofreaders work there?)

Correct spelling is still required in all online writing, mainly for credibility purposes. If you're talking about any topic with your online writing and you spell words incorrectly, you *don't look very smart* (like this guy)

What makes it worse is that spell check is readily available and you didn't bother to use it.

But what about those words that spell check couldn't catch because the error is still a real word? In those cases, you have to know the word you're trying to use or again, your **credibility** on the entire topic comes into question.

Three purposes of accurate spelling

1. **To convey the intended word**, showing basic intelligence of having a decent vocabulary

   e.g. *"bazaar"* when *"bizarre"* was intended

   "His behavior yesterday was rather bazaar." (It's bizarre that the actual person who wrote this in an legit email never recognized her blatant error, sheesh... Result: loss of all credibility.)

2. **To avoid distracting the reader**, taking the focus off the writing and onto the mistake

   e.g. *"their"* for *"they're"*

"I hope their coming with us tomorrow." *('their', 'they're',* and *'there'* are homonyms)

3. An open display of the writer's character (carelessness, rushing through → dependable? sloppy?)

e.g. *"currant"* for *"current"*; *"no"* for *"not"*

"Here is the currant data, no in the same format, but accurate." (but lacking proofreading accuracy)

Proofread, proof again, then proof yet again!

Hoot note: *Have a 3rd party proof really important writing pieces, since it's hard to proof our own work. We see what we expect to see, not the errors.*

17

A final note on spelling, you're probably not lucky enough to be the next google, who made up a catchy new name (plus verb form) due to a spelling error

googol* *(plan)* *google (error)*

[***googol** – a unit represented by the number 1 followed by 100 zeros, representing the vast internet]

RULE: Keep it SHORT – short words, short sentences, short paragraphs

When writing online to be read, short is IN - long is OUT. The main reason to keep it short is to make it scannable. In the busy world of digital communication it must be scannable, easily and quickly readable.

With long writing content there are fluency issues, rambling awkward constructions that not only require time and mental energy to get through, but also make the understanding process more difficult.

It's much harder to be short and concise then it is to ramble. So gather your thoughts concisely.

Short Sentences

Bullets are the preferable form to get across multiple items/ideas in list format.

Incomplete sentences are perfectly acceptable, often preferable.

Let's plan to table that issue and meet next week, perhaps on Tuesday, when we can really tackle such a meaty topic head-on, fully prepared, with our batteries fully charged and ready to do battle.

Let's reconvene next week. Come prepared. Tuesday good?

Taking this 35-word sentence down to 7 words, inside of three short sentences, is definitely the way to go. The conciseness, the clarity, maintaining full content is a joy for the reader to breeze through instead of being bogged down unnecessarily.

Short Words

Aim for three-syllable max words; look carefully to change words that go over three syllables to a comparable substitute.

aphrodisiac - love help
metamorphosis – change
community – group

Short Paragraphs

Each complete sentence can be its own paragraph, leaving lots of white space to the reader's eye. There is nothing more taxing with reading online writing then seeing a large block of text.

Break up all that text into one sentence paragraphs, and where possible keep the format to five sentences max.

If you feel the need to make email go over five sentences in length, consider picking up the phone to relay the information instead of sending a long email that may not even be read. And if it is read, it will likely not be fully digested and understood, without the opportunity to immediately ask clarifying questions.

In short, keeping things short serves three purposes:

> ➤ **There's a greater chance of being read and understood by the intended audience**

> ➤ **There's a greater chance of the content being processed accurately**

> ➤ **Being scannable saves the reader valuable time**

RULE: It's okay to begin a sentence with 'and' or 'but'

But - you promised...
And then SHE said...

More on '*and*' and '*but*':

"*And*" is additive; it adds to what is already written or said (the default conjunction)

We can do this, and that, and also this, AND...

"*And*" is softer, leans towards agreement. From a context point of view, if you want to be persuasive, get in the habit of changing the "but"s to "and"s and everyone is happier:

23

You did a great job with that report but I noticed it was a little late.

You did a great job with that report and I noticed it was a little late

Sounds very different with just the one word substitution.

***"But"* is diminishing;** it takes away from what was previously written or said. Sometimes it's even asked for, *"Thanks for the compliment - where's the 'but'?"* or *"OK…..but….?"*, *"I feel a 'but' coming…"*

However, when mental confusion is desirable, "but" is the word of choice to do the job:

Yes, that's true, but have you thought to consider…?

RULE: It's okay to end a sentence with a preposition

It's over.

Say goodbye to the clunky grammar rules of yesterday - today it's fine to end a sentence with a preposition. Nice and *short*.

RULE: It's okay to split infinitives

OK to split infinitives?!! OMG, are all the old traditions are falling by the wayside? But wait a minute – first, what's an 'infinitive' anyway??

Actually, few people actually know what it means to split an infinitive, only that they were told in grammar class not to do it.

An infinitive is "*to*" plus a verb: i.e. "*to walk*", "*to run*" etc. And it's absolutely fine to split them with an adverb between: "*to briskly walk*", "*to quickly run*".

The dated thinking was that the adverb should modify the verb - "*to walk briskly*", "*to run quickly*" - coming after the verb rather than splitting the infinitive construction, but who cares really?

To boldly go where no man (or grammarian) *has gone before*

RULE: It's okay to have incomplete sentences
(horrors!),

It's okay to have intentional fragments
(double horrors!),

It's okay to have verb-less sentences *(No! whatever is this world coming to?!)*

Hoping for some answers.

Enough.

Truly immortal.

The usage of a verb-less structure can serve several good purposes –

- it swings the writer's voice to informality
- it highlights important content details the writer wants to emphasize

27

- it focuses the reader on a key point
- it provides relief from long blocks of text
- it intensifies meaning
- it shocks the reader, gets noticed

 __Hoot Note__: Breaking these 3 rules especially helps make online writing stand out and gain wanted attention.

RULE: Headlines Rule - focus your major attention on them

While the content of the writing is your primary interest, however if the piece never gets opened or read, then all that good writing is wasted.

Headlines/subject titles do 80% of the work: 8 out of 10 people will read a headline, but only 2 of the 8 will move on to read the content of the email, the article, the white paper, etc. when the headline doesn't grab them as worthy of their valuable time and attention.

The headline must be specifically tailored to the audience's specific interest -

Stocks Hit Pause after a Record Run

For a Long Life, It Takes a Village

Words carry tone, which is determined by the reader, not the writer. Headline tone should be determined by the product/service; serious subjects → serious headlines –

The Horror of Boko Haram

Light subjects → fun, humorous headlines -

Eat ALL Of Your Vegetables
(an article on eating every part – roots, leaves, etc – of a vegetable)

29

A headline should tell the full story,

not leave the reader guessing -

Something Good Inside...

(this email is likely headed to trash unopened – a little mystery trick, but who has time for guessing games?)

Better headline examples that tell the full story of what's to come:

The Information You Requested

Thinking About Buying a Home Abroad?

The headline defines and selects the appropriate reader from the overall market –

Lessons from a Buffett Believer

Why Outlets Are No Bargain

A headline's **main job is to move the reader into the body** content

A Mom's Ad Seeks Groom for Her Son (re: a family in India)

Parents Hate School Too

All this work to do in only a few seconds; the headline must grab the reader's attention before they're gone. Remember, headlines do 80% of the work; they are critically important to getting online content noticed, so choose your headline carefully, if you want your online writing to actually be read, which I'm betting you do!

For more specific headline support, check out the accompanying resource *Headline Template COMPLETE Guide,* which not only gives you numerous successful headline templates to pick from, but also explains how to choose which template to use for your specific purpose.

Standard Grammar BASICS Brush-up

• Word and Sentence Construction Helps

➤ Remember this little ditty? It's a good one:

"*i*" before "*e*", except after "*c*", and when sounding like "*ay*", as in "*neighbor*" and "*weigh*"

receive, receipt (these follow the basic *exception* rule but seem to give people trouble)

believe, relief (these follow the basic rule)

'weird' (remembering that 'weird' is weird, and so it doesn't follow the basic rule)

> ## ➢ With a compound subject deciding between '*so-and-so and me*' or '*so-and-so and I*'? – simply take the other person out, then go with your ear.

Obama: "*Thank you for the warm welcome you gave Michelle and I.*"

No, no, Mr. President, it's "...*Michelle and me*" Notice that when you take Michelle out, it becomes clear, "*Thank you for the warm welcome you gave me.*"

Or, this also works: "***Michelle and I would like to thank you for the warm welcome***", since taking Michelle out would leave "***I*** *would like to thank you for the warm welcome.*"

Sometimes your ear is right which then makes the technically correct grammar 'wrong' (see Hyper Grammar above), as in this movie title:

33

Me and Earl and the Dying Girl

If you take out Earl, you're left with Me and You/the Dying Girl, which is commonly used, but is technically faulty construction, correctly it is: You/The Dying Girl and I, which doesn't flow off the tongue very well.

"The Dying Girl, Earl and I" doesn't have the nice flow that "Me and Earl and the Dying Girl" has, plus 'Earl' and 'Girl' rhyme, which gives the title even better flow. Let's leave hyper grammar by the wayside, shall we (see the first rule)?

➢ When deciding which indefinite article to use: **If the word begins with a** vowel sound**, use** *'an'***, otherwise use** *'a'* –

A historic event vs *An historic event*

People were taught that 'an' precedes an opening vowel sound, so they apply that rule to 'historic', somehow thinking that the 'h' is silent (?), but that is simply incorrect. The confusion on this is unnecessary, since your ear tells you that '*a historic event*' is smoother sounding with the 'a' vowel followed by the consonant sound of 'h' in 'historic'. If the 'h' was actually silent, "*an istoric event*" would be correct!

Other examples of initial consonants that have an opening vowel sound, so needs 'an' not 'a' are:

an FAQ ('e'vowel sound, as in 'effort')

an heir ('a' vowel sound, as in its homonym 'air')

an honor ('o' vowel sound, as in 'on')

an MRI ('e' sound, as in 'empty')

an NBA player ('a' sound, as in 'an')

an '80s look (obvious 'e' sound, as in 'eight')

➢ When to double the final consonant: **When adding an ending that starts with a vowel, double the last consonant**

COMMIT**:**
commit**ment**
commit**ted**
commit**ting**

The same basic rule as above - look to the letter that the ending begins with and double or don't double the base word's final consonant accordingly.

• Verbs – VOICE

Verbs are sorted into only one of three voice categories:

PASSIVE voice - the emphasis is on the receiver of the action

Take me out to the ballgame. Excuse me.

*ACTIVE voice - the subject performs the action

I'm going to the ballgame. I want to be excused.

Or it's a **LINKING** verb - usually linked by a form of the verb *to be, see, appear* - with no action and no relationship between the subject and predicate.

He is watching the ballgame. You're excused.

 Hoot Note: Writing in the active voice serves to move the reader to take action!

37

• Verbs – TENSE

In addition to voice, verbs also have tense

PRESENT tense - has immediacy
to it, urgency, the reader is witness to
events which can linger in the reader's
memory. But since the events are being
described currently, there is a dreamlike
quality to the action.

When I say now, I mean right now!

PAST tense - is more compelling,
the reader is watching the action unfolds
as a re-creation a past reality. This is a
vicarious experience for the reader reliving
the action with the subject of the story.

He screamed at her, "I said right now!"

MIXED past and present tense - only done inside a historical

past quote in narrative form, recording it as it happened at time, which was present tense when it happened. Otherwise, don't mix your tenses.

I heard him scream, "I mean right now!"

- # Verb/Subject Agreement

Verbs and subjects must be in agreement.

SINGULAR – one subject, verb form also singular

*He rides **off into the sunset.***

PLURAL - plural subject, verb agreement

*They ride **off into the sunset.***

39

Problematic subjects - which verb is correct?

Everyone rides *off into the sunset*

or ...

Everyone, ride *off into the sunset* -??

Technically one is a singular subject which takes the singular verb of "*rides*". But you could also argue that everyone is a plural subject, since there's more than one person involved, before it should be a plural form of the verb, which would be "*ride*".

Go back to hyper grammar; both are correct and you would not be wrong to use either one that sounds right.

Writing Extras

EXCLAMATIONS

~~emoticons~~ !

➕ Using an occasional exclamation point is acceptable, however avoid using emoticons - only if you want to be taken seriously.

Have a great weekend! ☺
(Hmm…too much with both)

➕ If the content has its own excitement or emotional intensity, no exclamation point are needed -

The date is coming right up-next Friday!!
The date is coming right up-next Friday.

- **Serious content** → limited exclamation points

I missed your call...! An emergency came up that couldn't be helped!! ☹

I missed your call - an emergency came up that couldn't be helped.

- **Less serious** content → more liberal with the exclamation points

Oops, sorry! ☹ Duh, my bad!!! Ciao ;-)

(too much for professionalism)

- The best use of an exclamation point is **after a quote** or dialogue that expresses excitement

She said, "I'm really excited to meet her"!

Hoot Note: Use "!" sparingly, one exclamation point per email is best, to maintain professionalism.

• PERIOD Power

More periods = more stops = slows down the reader's pace.

The key when using numerous periods to best affect is to avoid being abrupt in the writing.

Skillful use of periods can –

- o create suspense
- o explain step-by-step
- o magnify an emotion

He glided into the room. Very slowly. On tiptoes. Softly. Barely breathing.

• ACRONYMS/Initials

Acronyms are simple shorthand used to **exclude outsiders.** Initially acronyms only included initial letters that could be pronounced as a word (i.e. **BASE** jumping, with BASE standing for the different fixed structures to leap from - buildings, antennas, spans, earth - in the sport of jumping;

ARM - *adjustable-rate mortgage*

Some of these old acronyms have since been absorbed into language and become words their own right, losing the identity as an acronym

'snafu' **came from** *'situation normal, all f**ked/fouled up'*

Other acronyms remain initials only and are part of the lexicon in their initial formats, greatly enhanced by text messaging, easy shortcut communication.

LOL
IMHO
IRA

When using acronyms in writing, take care not to hinder the reader's understanding.

Does every reader know what that acronym that you think is in common usage – **ROFL** - exactly means? Do they have the same understanding of the acronym being used in the right context? (**IRA** - is that an" individual retirement account", or the "Irish Republican Army"?) Or you risk putting them on the outside, which is insulting and distances the reader…

• SLANG/Jargon

Slang and jargon are nonstandard English that should be used sparingly to create special effects in writing.

Let's invest CMOs and EFTs into the IRA ASAP!

Jargon can create an instant insider bond with the reader, making the reader feel warm and fuzzy for being on the inside.

However if the reader doesn't understand the jargon being used, the opposite effect can happen making the reader feel left out in the cold.

If you use nonstandard English and you're really not versant, you could come across looking foolish if your usage is wrong in even a slight way.

The authenticity that's lacking will show through, backfiring into a credibility issue.

So if you're using slang or jargon, be sure to know it thoroughly, use it well, but sparingly since you don't know the full extent of the reader's knowledge base.

• TABOO Words

Hell, go ahead and swear all you want, see if I give a damn!

An appropriate use of 'rough language' is in directly quoted speech, for realism.

Outside of that, know that personal use of consistent swear words defines the character of the user, as a strong reflection on personal branding, which is OK if that's the branding you want to be known for. But swearing is a poor reflection on professionalism.

However, used sparingly, taboo words have can have the multiple purposes:

- to **deflate pretension**

- as an occasional **shock** vehicle; definitely gets attention

Better alternatives to swearing to get similar results are to use *euphemisms, hyperbole, metaphors.*

• Figures of Speech –

Figures of speech are devices that create comparative association between a complex subject and something familiar. They are the best devices to explain hard to understand concepts in relation to familiar concepts that are easily understood.

➢ SIMILE

A simile is a direct comparison using the word "like" or "as"

She looked just like a little doll.

As rare as vegans at a pig roast.

➢ METAPHOR

The metaphor identifies two elements, without using the words "like" or "as". By hooking two different concepts together, a metaphor can be extremely powerful to bridge understanding, so the reader understands very quickly the meaning that the writer intends, when the familiar metaphor concept is used.

Formal? Ha, that wedding was a zoo.

You delivered a Grand Slam with that report.

You little devil, you.

➢ ANALOGY

An analogy is a device that includes both comparison and contrast, a shortened story.

He only ran 3 miles but the effort to navigate the steep hills made the run seem much further.

• ABSTRACT/CONCRETE

All descriptive words exist on an imaginary line of **abstract** (*happiness*) on one side to **concrete** that describes examples (*April 11, 1979 when our first child was born*) on the other side.

Abstractions are categories of ideas -
couture fashion

Concrete words give specific examples of broad abstractions -

i.e. a gold accented beaded top coupled with suede

49

boots (a specific example of couture fashion)

To gain full understanding of the concept, the reader often needs to move up or down the abstract/concrete line.

When moving from abstract to concrete, the reader is looking for clarification to better understand the idea -

What is an example of what's being talked about?

When moving from concrete abstract, the reader sees the singular instance, but needs to understand the tie in to the big conceptual idea -

from the specific (particular) → to the general (crowd)

 Hoot Note: **Good writing moves from the concrete 'showing' - giving detailed persuasive evidence of proof - to the abstract 'telling' - allowing the reader room to draw his own conclusions.**

• AMBIGUITY

When skillfully used, ambiguity can be a creative force, utilizing multiple wordplay meanings.

However, it's more typical for **unintentional ambiguity to create confusion**, obscure meaning, resulting in unwanted double entendres.

While these headlines are humorous, they are best to be avoided, as clear intentional writing is preferable to having your writing laughed at.

Sources of negative ambiguity include:

- **Homonyms** - when a word has multiple meanings there is room for ambiguity

Natives Eat Dogs, Bark

In this example the natives diet includes dogs and tree bark, but this condensed headline is not clearly expressed, due to the multiple meaning of the word "bark"

- **Same word** with different sentence constructions –

"Me Before You"

This ambiguous book title had me, like most others, thinking it referred to '*me, ahead of you*', when actually the author explained that the reference was to '*me- what I was like - before I met you*'. Ok!

- **Close word placement** - words with disparate meaning become ambiguous when closely placed –

Slowdown Continues to Accelerate

- **Verb Prepositions** – preposition choice modifying the verb creates confusion

Crowd Marches Over Six-Year-Old Death

- **Connotations** - words can have various connotations to take into consideration

Native American Students Well Endowed

The SmartyPants Secret on: Online GRAMMAR

If it sounds right to the well-tuned ear, go with it.

'Wrong" isn't necessarily wrong, as grammatically wrong is trumped by being socially right (everyone else understands it that way).

The old grammar rules do not hold fully for the new Internet Age - EXCEPT *spelling*, which still counts 100% – otherwise on grammar, go with what sounds natural, what is in common usage versus what is technically grammatically correct.

Write in a friendly conversational active voice (like talking to a friend over coffee) + incorporate the new rules, of which the most important is to make online writing *scannable*, and short, to save online reader's time.

Short words, short sentences, short paragraphs is relatable writing that will connect effectively. Really.

55

Book Bonus

As a thank you to buyers, there is an additional free resource available only to book buyers. Did you get yours? If you missed it, go to www.SmartyPantsSecrets.com/bookbonus.

It's has additional valuable content and is free to book buyers, so don't miss out on getting yours!

About Me

I am DR Martin, PhD* (*Personal human Development expertise) – Dolley Rapoport Martin. I took Dolley as my first name* in honor of the great First Lady Dolley Madison, whom I admire for her heroic actions in the White House during very turbulent times.

I took Rapoport as a middle name* in honor of Ingeborg Rapoport, who at age 103, is the oldest person to be awarded a Doctorate; finally getting the recognition due her from 77 years prior in Nazi Germany, unfairly denied her due to her Jewish roots. There is so much injustice in the world; it is an honor to recognize her achievement by taking her name.

*[*The selecting of one's name is an important exercise, since names are so personal and tied to identity. Yet most of us go through life with a name not of our choosing. Check out the SmartyPants Secret book NAMES and NAMING for more on this subject.]*

I have a mind that is ever curious about so many topics. I have earned multiple expert designations (education certified

English teacher, Real Estate Broker, Stock Broker series 7, series 6, series, Certified Financial Manager, Insurance producer certified, Coach University) and held high level positions in business – large corporate entities, privately held companies, non-profit organizations, and startups – and have volunteered extensively, holding executive positions at the local, district and national levels. So I've been around the block more than once, on more than one topic.

I have also studied every communication subject for more than a decade, acquiring a large body of knowledge. I, perhaps like you, am a voracious reader and learner. My other strength is that I retain much of what I learn, so I can then compile the knowledge on a variety of subjects into a concise format, making the books that I author a shortcut on the best knowledge available.

This saves you from going through all the data looking for the kernel that makes the greatest difference in success, the SmartyPants secret on a given topic.

Due to my research and experience, I have

logged the perquisite time to carry the title of expert, giving myself an honorary PhD in the expertise area of communication, Personal human Development. I am passionate about sharing the knowledge that I have gained with you, in bite-size pieces.

And when a certain topic is not in my field of expertise, I find an expert with deep expertise in the field who has the knowledge that I seek. I then ask numerous in-depth questions of the expert to get to the gist, to learn the SmartyPants Secret on their expert topic, to then pass it on, in a book on the subject.

For other titles and additional resources, visit
www.SmartyPantsSecrets.com ,

Content clips and tips on a variety of topics at
www.youtube.com/c/smartypantssecrets

Contact: info@SmartyPantsSecrets.com